T0021151

Arabic Character Writing

by Keith Massey, PhD
and Damien Ferré

for
dummies®
A Wiley Brand

Arabic Character Writing For Dummies®

Published by: **John Wiley & Sons, Inc.,** 111 River Street, Hoboken, NJ 07030-5774, www.wiley.com

Copyright © 2020 by John Wiley & Sons, Inc., Hoboken, New Jersey

Published simultaneously in Canada

For general information on our other products and services, please contact our Customer Care Department within the U.S. at 877-762-2974, outside the U.S. at 317-572-3993, or fax 317-572-4002. For technical support, please visit https://hub.wiley.com/community/support/dummies.

Wiley publishes in a variety of print and electronic formats and by print-on-demand. Some material included with standard print versions of this book may not be included in e-books or in print-on-demand. If this book refers to media such as a CD or DVD that is not included in the version you purchased, you may download this material at http://booksupport.wiley.com. For more information about Wiley products, visit www.wiley.com.

Library of Congress Control Number: 2019948866

ISBN 978-1-119-47533-0 (pbk); ISBN 978-1-119-47559-0 (ebk); ISBN 978-1-119-47558-3 (ebk)

Manufactured in the United States of America

SKY10034520_052022

Table of Contents

Introduction

You're holding this book because you want to learn how to write the Arabic alphabet — and there are so many good reasons to learn this valuable skill! As I'll explain in more depth later, the Arabic alphabet is not just the script used to write the fifth-most spoken language in the world, Arabic, but it is also used to write several other languages, such as Farsi (Persian) and Kurdish, to name just a couple.

Your biggest challenge, and one that this book will help you overcome, is that the various letters of the Arabic alphabet have different shapes, depending on where they fall in a word. This adds not only to the beauty and variety of the writing system but also to the complexity you must master.

Like everything in life, practice makes perfect. This book will give you abundant opportunities to learn and practice writing the characters of the Arabic alphabet until you are comfortable and satisfied with your newfound skills!

About This Book

In this book you will learn the 28 characters of the Arabic alphabet, as well as a handful of additional symbols used to indicate things like the short vowels and doubled letters. The 28 characters include 27 consonants, which means that Arabic has a number of consonants that English simply does not possess. No worries, the sounds behind these new consonants will be explained to you.

You will discover that each of the 28 characters takes on a slightly different shape, depending on where exactly in the word the character appears — at the beginning, middle, or end. You will also become an expert in how the letters may or may not connect to one another.

Foolish Assumptions

This book is intended for someone who has absolutely no prior contact with the Arabic alphabet or language. That said, it will still be a valuable resource for people with some previous experience who want to brush up on their skills. Nevertheless, as I write this book, the audience I have in mind is starting from scratch.

Icons Used in This Book

The following icons appear periodically in the book to highlight important points to help you succeed in your mission of mastering the characters of the Arabic alphabet.

REMEMBER This icon will point out particularly important information to commit to memory.

TIP Be on the lookout for this icon to get helpful pointers on how to form the characters with the greatest ease and efficiency.

WARNING This icon will flag some of the most common mistakes that people tend to make.

Where to Go from Here

My recommendation to you is that you carefully read the information in Chapter 1 so that you understand very well the concepts of the independent, initial, medial, and final letters of the Arabic alphabet, as well as the issue of the one- and two-directional connectors. As soon as you have studied the first three letters, you will have the opportunity to practice writing entire words. A mastery of the different forms and how you join them will be crucial to making the most out of that practice.

As I have said, practice makes perfect. I supply you with space to practice the letters, but you should fill entire notebooks with additional practice on everything you discover here.

Now, if you are ready to accept your mission, turn the page and begin your journey into the fulfilling world of writing the Arabic alphabet!

Chapter **1**

Wrapping Your Mind around the Characters of the Arabic Alphabet

A frequent reaction when seeing Arabic writing is to note how simply beautiful it is. It is composed of flourishing shapes, joined delicately to one another. Unfortunately, as with all worthy things, it is not easy to learn how to form and connect these letters. In this book, however, I make it as painless for you as possible. When you have worked your way through this book, you will be writing the beautiful Arabic alphabet like a pro.

I walk you step by step through the different characters and give you my personal advice on how to cherish and succeed in this learning experience.

A Brief History of the Arabic Language and Its Alphabet

Arabic is a member of the Semitic language family, which includes Hebrew, Aramaic, and Amharic, which are still spoken today, as well as a number of ancient languages, such as Moabite and Phoenician. Semitic languages are characterized by the use of *triliteral roots* (words with the same three consonants with variations on the root meaning). So, for example, the word *kataba* means "to write," *kitaab* means "book," *kaatib* means "writer," and *maktaba* means "library."

The Arabic alphabet as we know it today evolved from the Nabataean alphabet, which was in use in the northwest corner of Arabia during the early centuries of the Common Era (CE). The Arabic language and alphabet gained significant importance through the legacy of the Prophet Muhammad (circa 570 CE to 632 CE). As Islam spread from the Arabian Peninsula in the seventh and eighth centuries CE, the language and writing system used for the Qur'an replaced others throughout the Middle East and North Africa.

In the centuries following the spread of Islam, Arabic evolved into a number of local dialects. As a general rule, these dialects are mutually intelligible to their neighbors, but not much farther. In other words, a native speaker of Egyptian Arabic can get by with a Libyan, a Libyan can get by with an Algerian, but an Egyptian cannot follow very colloquial Algerian with ease. The good news is they don't need to understand each other's dialects. Owing to the importance of the Qur'an in Islamic culture, the classical form of the language remains a *lingua franca* throughout the Arab world. Known as Fusha or Modern Standard Arabic, this formal register of speech is used for news broadcasts and official documents and serves as the mode of speech when Arabic speakers from different regions want to communicate apart from their respective dialects.

REMEMBER

While each country or region in the Arab world speaks a dialect with its own particular traits, Modern Standard Arabic, understood by all educated Arabs, is the language of mass media and provides a neutral register of speech that unifies the region.

What? No Vowels?

Originally Arabic was written with no short vowels. You might think it impossible for a language to function without them, but take a look at the following:

Tmrrw th wthr shld b bttr thn tdy.

You probably read that with little hesitation as "Tomorrow the weather should be better than today." Because of the context, the fact that the word *thn* could represent both "than" and "then" did not confuse you.

Newspapers and online news in Arabic do not use any short vowels. Native speakers have no problem reading without them, even though there are many situations like the word *thn* demonstrated here. Context makes the correct reading clear. Nevertheless, a system of short vowel symbols was developed in order to make some texts, in particular the Qur'an, readable for people who were not to mention all the other issues that short vowels clear up, such as passive vs. active voice! A full description of these symbols is included in this book as well.

Connecting the Different Forms of the Letters

One thing that makes the Arabic script difficult is that the various letters may or may not connect to other letters both before and after themselves. Don't worry, this is not guesswork. There are firm rules you will learn that govern how you connect the letters. This book will also give you abundant practice in writing and connecting them correctly.

Arabic letters that can be connected only to letters on their own right side are called *one-directional connectors*. There are other letters that can connect to letters on both their right and their left sides. These are called, predictably enough, *two-directional connectors*. The shape and appearance of the letters can be different, depending on where you use them in a word. Two-directional connectors have a total of four possible shapes; one-directional connectors have two. Here is a description of all the potential forms of the letters that you will be learning.

>> **Independent:** The form of the letter that stands alone, unconnected to any other letter. One-directional connectors also use this form as the initial form, because they cannot connect to a following letter. A two-directional connector uses this form when it is the last letter in a word and directly follows a one-directional connector.

>> **Initial:** The form of the letter when it starts a word. One-directional connectors use the same shape for initial and independent forms. Two-directional letters have an initial form that is different from the independent form.

>> **Medial:** The form of the letter when it appears in the middle of a word.

>> **Final:** The form of the letter when it is the last letter of a word. If the final form follows a one-directional connector, it is identical to the independent form. One-directional connectors use the same form for final as they do for medial. Two-directional connectors use a unique form when they are the last letter of the word and connect to a preceding two-directional connector.

Let me demonstrate how this works. Here are two Arabic letters, the *daal* followed by the *'alif*:

دا

The *daal* and the *'alif* are both one-directional connectors. For that reason, you would use the initial form of the *daal*, followed by the initial form of the *'alif*.

But look at what happens if you put a two-directional connector before that *'alif*. If you now write the letter *baa'* (a two-directional connector) followed by an *'alif*, you use the medial form of the *'alif*:

با

Again, remember that two-directional connectors can connect on both their right and left sides. But they only do so if they are preceded and followed by other two-directional connectors. Here is an example of three letters thus connected, the Arabic word for "camel," *jamal*:

Why Learn to Write Arabic?

You might have a number of reasons for learning to write the Arabic alphabet. If you want to learn the Arabic language, the alphabet is essential, because no country or region uses the Latin alphabet to write it (with the single curious exception of Malta). If you are a Muslim who wants to read your religion's Holy Book in the original language, a knowledge of the Arabic alphabet is a necessity.

Simply put, if you want to enter into the fullness of the beauty and richness of Arab culture and literature, you need to learn to read and write the Arabic alphabet. This book will help you achieve that worthy goal.

Strategies for Learning to Write Arabic Letters

My advice to you is to use this book regularly and systematically. Master the concept of the one- and two-directional connectors described earlier. Study your way to a comfortable command of the different shapes of the individual letters and how they connect to one another.

Do not skimp on practice. The space provided for practicing the characters should be fully used. Don't just practice the letter two or three times and decide you are done. In fact, a valuable strategy would be to practice a letter two or three times and then go back and practice that same letter two or three times every single day as you continue learning new letters in this book.

In addition to the work you will do in this book, take a look at Arabic writing in some other source, such as a newspaper, whether online or in print. Study the text and observe how the various letters connect and why they have the shapes they do in their context within the word. This will also make you more adept at recognizing the letters in a font that is different from the one I use in this book.

Set goals

As I have said more than once already, practice makes perfect. When people learn that I can easily read and write the Arabic alphabet, I remember the dozens of hours of practice that led up to having that skill. I don't mean to scare you off, but at the same time I don't want to mislead you. The Arabic alphabet is significantly more difficult than the Latin alphabet. In the Latin alphabet, every letter is what it is regardless of where it appears in a word, and letters don't connect to one another (except in cursive writing, of course). As you have already encountered, the Arabic alphabet includes different forms and letters that do and do not connect to others. You will master this skill through regular practice, writing the letters and words that include the letters.

Here are some strategies to help you achieve your desired result:

>> Practice for a set number of minutes every single day. I am a firm believer in the philosophy that something is always better than nothing. If you decide to practice for 15 minutes a day, that would be a good goal. If some days you can't find even 15 minutes, do something, rather than nothing.

>> Make your practice cumulative; repractice letters you have already studied on a regular basis so that you continue to master them.

>> Look back over what you have practiced as a way to encourage yourself at how far you have come!

Chapter **2**

The Write Stuff

In this chapter, before diving into learning and practicing 100 characters, I cover some of the more practical matters that you will face when writing (and reading) the Arabic alphabet. And before you actually start learning and practicing how to write, I help you choose the best equipment for the job.

Traditional Writing Utensils and Mediums

Thousands of years ago, when the Arabic alphabet as we know it was first invented, people carved the characters in stone and also painted them on a variety of materials. You heard me right: They painted them when they put them on more perishable materials than stone. According to Islamic sources, when the Qur'an was first compiled into one volume by the first Caliph Abu Bakr, it was drawn from sources recorded on materials such as leather, parchment, bones, and leaves. And these words would have been painted with black ink and a fine paintbrush.

A curious feature of these painted letters is that, originally, no one really cared which direction the letters went. Sometimes scribes would write from right to left, and then in the next line reverse direction and go from left to right! This practice is called *boustrophedon* writing, from the Greek for "ox plowing" (because, after all, when you plow a field, you just turn around at the end of the field and plow your way back to where you started).

People were either painting their letters or carving them in stone throughout the Middle East and the Mediterranean until the sixth century BCE, when the Greeks invented a split-reed pen that allowed ink to flow onto the writing material from a reservoir. Overnight, boustrophedon writing came to an end, and the direction of writing became locked in at left to right. Can you think of why? It all comes down to the fact that 90 percent of people are right-handed and the pen works best when pulled across the papyrus in a left-to-right direction.

REMEMBER

The tradition of using paintbrushes persisted, particularly on holy manuscripts such as the Torah and the Qur'an. It contributed to the development of Hebrew and Arabic eventually being codified into a right-to-left writing direction. Even today, a skilled Arabic calligrapher will work with a fine paintbrush instead of any type of pen.

Your Best Options — Pencil and Paper

When I was learning to write the Arabic alphabet, I found that the best instrument was a .05 mm mechanical pencil. The lead is large enough to produce the intricate shapes of the letters and the dots that accompany many of the letters. The .05 mm is also fine enough to allow the alphabet to be written even on single lines of a standard lined notebook.

TIP

That being said, for the practice sections of this book, you may want to use something larger and sturdier. I suggest the classic sharpened wooden pencil. You should use a pencil because you will make mistakes and you'll want to be able to erase them and correct yourself. Be sure to also practice writing the letters on a smaller scale in the practice sections, as in due time, you will want to have the skills to write an Arabic letter or note, just as you would in English.

I also recommend that you get a notebook with wide-ruled lines for additional practice beyond the space provided in this book. When you first start, skip every other line. This way, you will leave yourself a lot of room to comfortably add the various dots that appear with many of the letters, as well as the vowel signs.

A Fountain of Fonts

Just as Times New Roman doesn't look quite the same as Arial or Helvetica, a variety of both online and publishing fonts are used for the Arabic language. In this book, I have selected Markazi for you to use as the basis for your practice in writing. Markazi matches very nicely the types of strokes and loops that traditionally handwritten Arabic uses. Even so, I would like to show you some of the different fonts you may encounter as you begin reading Arabic. Look at the Arabic word for *Arabic* as it appears in a variety of fonts:

Markazi	العربية
Times New Roman Arabic	العربية
Traditional Arabic	العربية
Courier	العربية

As you can see, although the letters look more or less the same, there can be significant differences in style that lead to different shapes.

There's More than One Way to Write

For your convenience, I'm giving you numbers and arrows in this book to guide you as you practice writing the letters. That being said, no rules are written in stone for exactly how to form all of them. For example, one form of the letter *haa'* (just like the English *h*) is basically a circle:

You will obviously start somewhere and draw a circular shape until you meet where you started. Early on, I learned to write this shape counterclockwise, and that is what I will show you when you get to that letter in the book. But there is no reason why you can't start somewhere else and go clockwise if that is more comfortable for you.

Likewise, the Arabic letter *kaaf* (just like the English *k*) has a unique shape that you can write in a variety of ways. When a *kaaf* starts a word, I write it as one continuous line, as follows:

But some people prefer to write the *kaaf* in other ways, as in the following example:

My point is that the numbers and arrows that I use are intended as guidelines to assist you, not to be followed, forgive the pun, to the letter of the law. What feels comfortable to you is what you should pursue, just as long as the end result is an Arabic letter that will be recognizable to others.

REMEMBER

Long Live Cursive Writing!

There is a debate among educators today as to whether cursive writing should still be formally taught and practiced by young students. As a teacher, I can assure you that a vast majority of my students do not use it at all, even if they know how to read it. Arabic writing, however, is exclusively cursive; there is no block-letter option whatsoever. As a result, you will shortly be learning (as with cursive writing in English) how you do and do not join the various letters together. I also want to show you some common variants that you will see only in handwritten Arabic.

In both typed fonts and the writing you will practice for this book, these two letters are formed with three loops (for the *siin*) and the addition of three dots (to produce the *shiin*):

A common handwritten variant for these letters is to replace the loops with a long, straight horizontal line. Also, instead of writing three dots, you may see a writer replace them with an upside-down *v* (which is a quick way to represent the three dots):

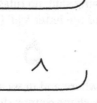

Writing the Arabic alphabet is truly more of an art than a science. My final advice in this chapter is to take the time to trace these flowing and beautiful shapes with care from the very beginning of your studies, not just so that they will be legible, but also to let your writing be a creative expression that you will find rewarding.

Write, review, rinse, repeat

Practice, practice, practice! When you have filled every available space in this book for practicing the letters, take a blank notebook and start all over by working your way through all the exercises once, twice, or three times again. Do all this, and the ability to read and write the Arabic alphabet will be yours; the rewards are substantial. Turn the page and resolve that you are going to study and practice the first letter — do it right now. I congratulate you in advance.

أَلِف • 'alif

The first letter of the Arabic alphabet, the *'alif*, represents the long *a* vowel (pronounced, depending on the letter that precedes it, as either the *a* in *glad* or the *a* in *car*). You will write the independent *'alif* as a single line downward. The final connected *'alif* is written upward from the letter it is connected to. (You will also learn later that the *'alif* is used with the symbol we call the *hamza*, which represents the glottal stop sound.) The top of the letter should be just below the line above it, and the bottom of the *'alif* should reach the line on which you are writing. Try writing the *'alif*:

Independent

Initial

Medial

Final

baa' • باء

The letter *baa'* is pronounced like the *b* in the English word *baby*. It's a two-directional connector, so it connects on its right and left sides, and therefore it has all four potential forms. The bottom of all the forms of the *baa'* should touch the bottom of the line on which you are writing. After writing the shape of the letter, you add a single dot below the character. Try them:

Independent

Initial

Medial

Final

تاء • taa'

The letter *taa'* is pronounced like the *t* in the English word *tame*. It's a two-directional connector, so it connects on its right and left sides, and therefore it has all four potential forms. The bottom of all the forms of the *taa'* should touch the bottom of the line on which you are writing. It uses the same forms as the *baa'*, except after writing the shape of the letter, you add two dots next to each other on top of the character. Try them:

Independent

Initial

Medial

Final

ثاء • thaa'

The letter *thaa'* is pronounced like the *th* in the English word *thin*. It's a two-directional connector, so it connects on its right and left sides, and therefore it has all four potential forms. The bottom of all the forms of the *thaa'* should touch the bottom of the line on which you are writing. It uses the same forms as the *baa'* and *taa'*, except after writing the shape of the letter, you add three dots in a triangular configuration above the character. Try them:

Independent

ث

Initial

ﺛ

Medial

ﺜ

Final

ﺚ

جمعة
مملكة
مستقلة
Independent
Initial
Medial
Final
Independent

Father اب

اب

باب Door

باب

ثابت Firm

ثابت

بث To broadcast

بث

بابا Daddy

بابا

jiim · جيم

The letter *jiim* is pronounced like the *j* in the English word *jam*. It's a two-directional connector, so it connects on its right and left sides, and therefore it has all four potential forms. The letter is formed with a sharp angle shape, as you can see below. The bottom of the initial and medial forms of *jiim* should touch the bottom of the line on which you are writing, whereas the independent and final forms are written half above and half below the line. After writing the shape of the letter, you add one dot below the character in the initial and medial forms, and in the center of the independent and final forms. Try them:

Independent

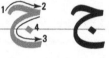

Initial

Medial

Final

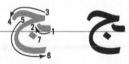

Bodies جثث

جثث

To answer اجاب

اجاب

Crown تاج

تاج

Wells اجباب

اجباب

Excuses حجج

حجج

haa' ‏حاء‏

The letter *haa'* represents a sound that does not occur in English. It is between the English *h* and the harder sound represented by the *ch* in the Scottish word *loch*. Perhaps the closest thing in English to the *Haa'* is the *h* in the word *hot*. It's a two-directional connector, using the same shape as the *jiim*, but without any dot. Try them:

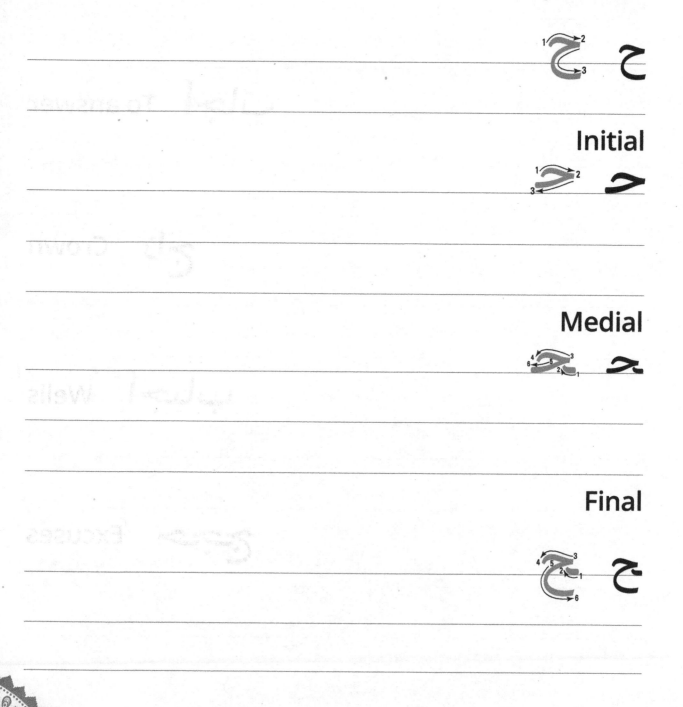

Independent

Initial

Medial

Final

Darlings   احباب

احباب

_____

Hijab   حجاب

حجاب

_____

To search for   بحث

بحث

_____

Pilgrim   حاج

حاج

_____

To become hoarse   بح

بح

_____

خاء • khaa'

The letter *khaa'* represents a hard *h* sound similar to what is represented by the *ch* in the Scottish word *loch*. It's a two-directional connector, using the same shape as the *jiim* and *haa'*, but with one dot above the letter. Try them:

Independent

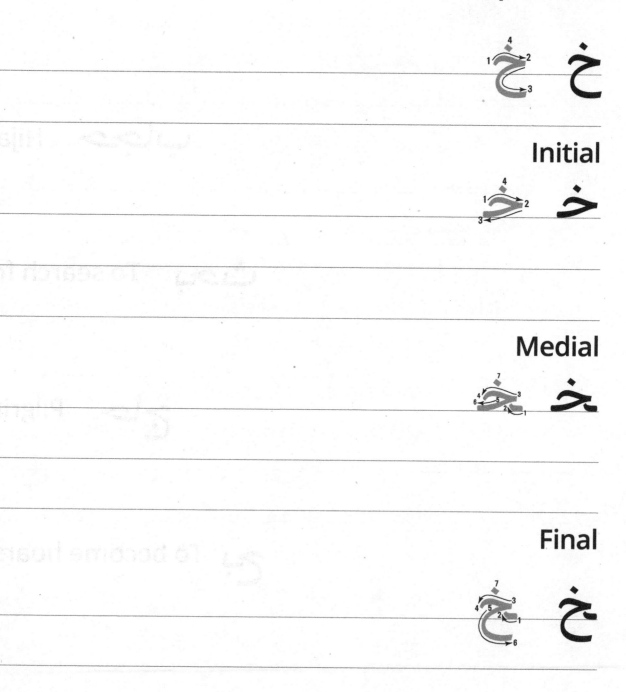

Initial

Medial

Final

The letter *daal* is pronounced as the *d* in *dad*. It joins in one direction only, to the letter to the right of it. The two connectors on the left of the letter joins it only to its own family. The bottom of the *daal* sits just above the base line, which you are writing your letters on.

Sister   اخت

اخت

Independent

Luck   بخت

بخت

Initial

To decay   تختخ

تختخ

Medial

Trot   خبب

خبب

Final

To boast   جخّ

جخّ

داد • daal

The letter *daal* is pronounced like the *d* in *doll*. It is a one-directional connector, so it connects to a two-directional connector only on its own right side. The form is written like a 45-degree angle pointing left. The bottom of the *daal* should just touch the line on which you are writing. Try them:

Independent

Initial

Medial

Final

Grandfather   جَدّ

جَدّ

Cheek   خَدّ

خَدّ

Bears   أدباب

أدباب

Chickens   دجاج

دجاج

Incident   حدث

حدث

dhaal • ذال

The letter *dhaal* is pronounced like the *th* in *this*. It is formed exactly like the *daal*, except you add a single dot above the letter. It is a one-directional connector, meaning it connects to a two-directional connector on its own right side. The bottom of the *dhaal* should just touch the line on which you are writing. Try them:

Independent

ذ

Initial

ذ

Medial

ذ

Final

ذ

Luxury	بذخ

بذخ

Flies	ذباب

ذباب

Attractive	جاذب

جاذب

Oscillation	تذبذب

تذبذب

To imitate	حذا

حذا

راء • raa'

The letter *raa'* is a trilled *r* such as you find in Spanish or Italian. It's a one-directional connector, connecting to two-directional connectors only on its own right side. As such, the independent form and the initial form are identical. The medial and final forms are also identical to each other. The form is drawn as a curved line pointing to the left. The bottom half of the *raa'* will be under the line on which you are writing. Try them:

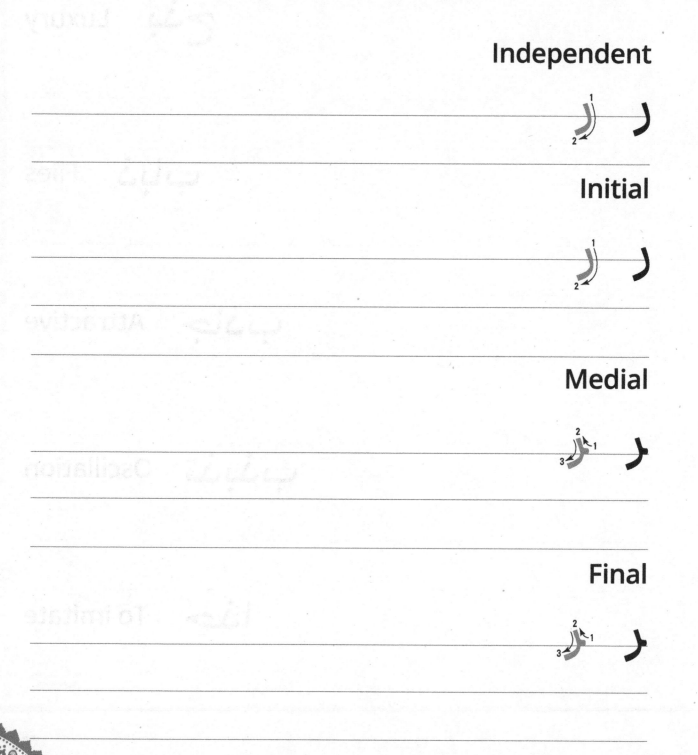

Independent

Initial

Medial

Final

War حرب

حرب

Information خبر

خبر

Cold برد

برد

To hope رجا

رجا

Hesitation تردّد

تردّد

زاي · zaay

The letter *zaay* is pronounced like the *z* in *zoo*. It is formed exactly like the *raa'* except you add one dot above the upper point of the character. It's a one-directional connector, connecting to two-directional connectors only on its own right side. As such, the independent form and the initial form are identical. The medial and final forms are also identical to each other. The bottom half of the *zaay* will be under the line on which you are writing. Try them:

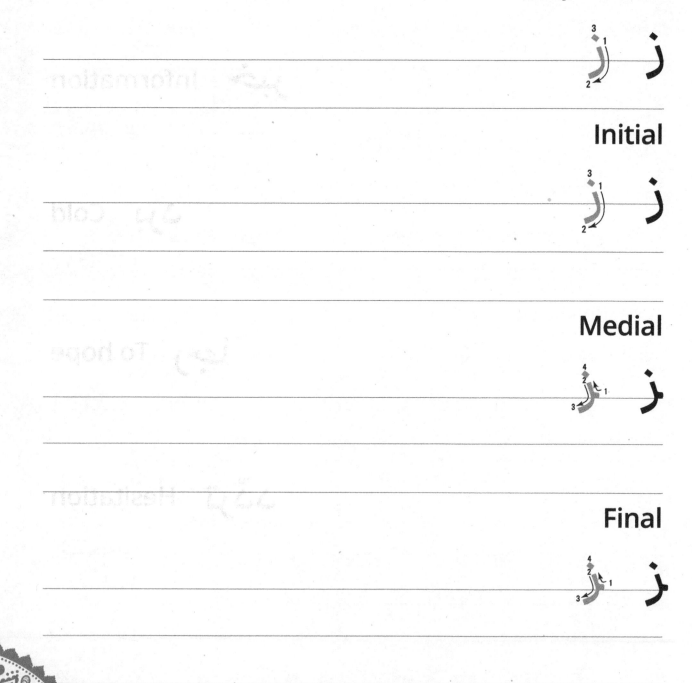

Independent

Initial

Medial

Final

To visit   زار

زار

Political Party   حزب

حزب

Bread   خبز

خبز

Glass   زجاج

زجاج

to chirp   زرزر

زرزر

siin · سين

The letter *siin* is pronounced like the *s* in the English word *same*. It's a two-directional connector, so it connects on its right and left sides, and therefore it has four different forms. It is written with two small hooks, as you can see below, plus one large hook at the end of the independent and final forms. The bottom of the initial and medial forms of the *siin* should touch the bottom of the line on which you are writing, while the independent form and the final form have a curve that will dip below the line of writing. Try them:

Independent

Initial

Medial

Final

Sixth   سادس

سادس

Lesson   درس

درس

According to   حسب

حسب

Bell   جرس

جرس

Bridge   جسر

جسر

shiin · شين

The letter *shiin* is pronounced like the *sh* in the English word *she*. It's formed exactly like the *siin* except you add three dots in a pyramid configuration over the two loops of the character. It's a two-directional connector, so it connects on its right and left sides, and therefore it has four different forms. The bottom of the initial and medial forms of the *shiin* should touch the bottom of the line on which you are writing, while the independent form and the final form have a curve that will dip below the line of writing. Try them:

Independent

Initial

Medial

Final

Trees شجر

شجر

To drink شرب

شرب

Good news بشر

بشر

To crush جرش

جرش

Wood خشب

خشب

saad • صاد

The letter *saad* represents a sound that does not occur in English. It is pronounced like a hard *s* sound, most similar to the sound in the English word *sauce*. It's a two-directional connector, so it connects on its right and left sides; and therefore it has four different forms. As you can see below, the main shape of the *saad* looks like a deflated balloon. The bottom of all the forms of the *saad* should touch the bottom of the line on which you are writing, whereas the independent form and the final form have a curve that will dip below the line of writing. Try them:

Independent

Initial

Medial

Final

Morning صباح

صباح

Patience صبر

صبر

Special خاصّ

خاصّ

Vision بصر

بصر

Bullets رصاص

رصاص

ضاد • daad

The letter *daad* represents a sound that does not occur in English. It is pronounced like a dull *d* sound, most similar to the *d* in daughter. It's formed exactly like the *saad* except you add one dot above the character. It's a two-directional connector, so it connects on its right and left sides, and therefore it has four different forms. The bottom of all the forms of the *daad* should touch the bottom of the line on which you are writing, while the independent form and the final form have a curve that will dip below the line of writing. Try them:

Independent

Initial

Medial

Final

Beating ضرب

ضرب

Against ضدّ

ضدّ

Green أخضر

أخضر

To incite حضّ

حضّ

Saliva رضاب

رضاب

طاء · taa'

The letter *taa'* represents a sound that does not occur in English. It is pronounced like a dull *t* sound, similar to a *t* sound you would make when spitting out the toothpaste after brushing your teeth. It's formed like the *saad* except you add a vertical line that touches the base of the letter on the left side, as you can see below. It's a two-directional connector, so it connects on its right and left sides, and therefore it has four different forms. The bottom of all the forms of the *taa'* should touch the bottom of the line on which you are writing. Try them:

Independent

Initial

Medial

Final

Medicine   طبّ

طبّ

To drive away   طرد

طرد

Surface   سطح

سطح

Condition   شرط

شرط

Line   خطّ

خطّ

ظاء · DHaa'

The letter *DHaa'* represents a sound that does not occur in English. It is pronounced like a cross between a dull *z* and *th* sound. It's formed exactly like the *taa'* except you add one dot above the character. It's a two-directional connector, so it connects on its right and left sides, and therefore it has four different forms. The bottom of all the forms of the *DHaa'* should touch the bottom of the line on which you are writing. Try them:

Independent

Initial

Medial

Final

ظرّ **Flint**

ظرّ

حظّ **Luck**

حظّ

حظر **Prohibition**

حظر

بظّ **To gush out**

بظّ

عين · 'ayn

The letter *'ayn* represents a sound not found in English. It is formed by tightening the back of the throat and then speaking a vowel through it. It's a two-directional connector, so it connects on its right and left sides, and therefore it has four different forms. The initial and medial forms have a shape like the letter C; the medial and final forms have a shape like an upside-down triangle, as you can see below. The bottom of all the forms of the *'ayn* should touch the bottom of the line on which you are writing. The independent form and the final form have a curve that will dip below the line of writing. Try them:

Independent

Initial

Medial

Final

Across عبر

عبر

Tenth عاشر

عاشر

Price سعر

سعر

To sell باع

باع

Seventh سابع

سابع

ghayn · غين

The letter *ghayn* represents a sound not found in English. It is like a *g* but it is a *fricative* letter, meaning it includes a raspy sound at the back of the throat. It is similar to the sound one makes when gurgling. It's formed exactly like the *'ayn* except you add one dot above the character. It's a two-directional connector, so it connects on its right and left sides, and therefore it has four different forms. The bottom of all the forms of the *ghayn* should touch the bottom of the line on which you are writing. The independent form and the final form have a curve that will dip below the line of writing. Try them:

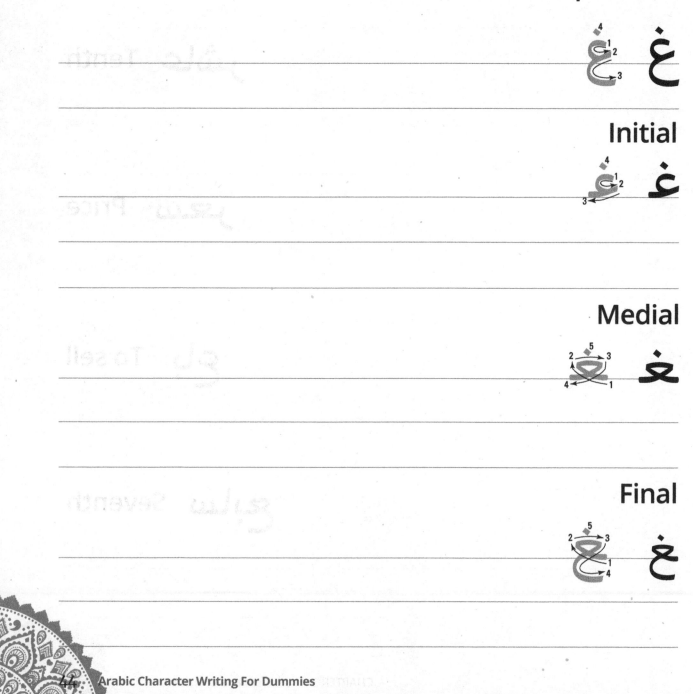

Independent

Initial

Medial

Final

ممارسة Practice

Gas غاز

غاز

_____

Attack دغر

دغر

_____

To desire رغب

رغب

_____

To surprise بغت

بغت

_____

Tanner دبّاغ

دبّاغ

_____

faa' • فاء

The letter *faa'* represents the same sound as the *f* in *fact*. It's a two-directional connector, so it connects on its right and left sides, and therefore it has four different forms. In all its forms it includes a small circular form, with one dot added above the form. This is so you can tell it apart from the similar form of the letter *miim*, which you will soon encounter. The bottom of all the forms of the *faa'* should touch the bottom of the line on which you are writing. Try them:

Independent

ف

Initial

ف

Medial

ف

Final

ف

Opening فتح

فتح

Glory فخر

فخر

Zero صفر

صفر

Dryness جفاف

جفاف

To shudder رجف

رجف

قاف · qaaf

The letter *qaaf* represents a sound not found in English. It is like a *k* sound but it is formed at the back of the throat. It's formed like the *faa'* except you add two dots above the character. Also, in the independent and final forms of the *qaaf*, you have a curve that dips below the line of writing, while the curves of the *faa'* stay above the line. It's a two-directional connector, so it connects on its right and left sides, and therefore it has four different forms. The bottom of all the forms of the *qaaf* should touch the bottom of the line on which you are writing. Try them:

Independent

ق

Initial

ق

Medial

ق

Final

ق

Destiny قدر

قدر

Cattle بقر

بقر

To drill ثقب

ثقب

East شرق

شرق

Friendliness رفق

رفق

كاف • kaaf

The letter *kaaf* is pronounced like the *k* in the English word *kiss*. It's a two-directional connector, so it connects on its right and left sides, and therefore it has four different forms. The bottom of all the forms of the *kaaf* should touch the bottom of the line on which you are writing. It is unique among the Arabic letters because the initial and medial forms have a very different shape and an s-like shape not found at all with the independent and final forms. Try them:

Independent

ك

Initial

ک

Medial

ک

Final

ك

Book   كتاب

كتاب

Thankfulness   شكر

شكر

To remember   ذكر

ذكر

To bless   بارك

بارك

To entwine   شبك

شبك

laam • لام

The letter *laam* is pronounced like the *l* in the English word *love*. Because it is formed with a single straight line, it is easily confused with the *'alif*. One important difference is that the *laam* is a two-directional connector, so it connects on its right and left sides, and therefore it has four different forms. The bottom of the initial and medial forms of the *laam* should touch the bottom of the line on which you are writing. The independent form and the final form have a curve that will dip below the line of writing. Try them:

Independent

Initial

Medial

Final

Meat لحم

لحم

Dog كلب

كلب

Heart قلب

قلب

Onion بصل

بصل

Mind بال

بال

مهارسة · Practice

miim · ميم

The letter *miim* is pronounced like the *m* in the English word *me*. It's a two-directional connector, so it connects on its right and left sides, and therefore it has all four potential forms. It is formed with a circular shape, which makes it similar to the *faa'* and the *qaaf*; however, the *miim* does not have any dots. The *miim* rests on the line of writing in its initial and medial forms and has a tail that hangs below the line of writing in the independent and final forms. Try them:

Independent

Initial

Medial

Final

Similar   مثل

Independent
مثل

ن

Moon   قمر

Initial
قمر

ن

Dates   تمر

تمر

Medial

Mouth   فم

فم

Final

Bathroom   حمّام

ن

حمّام

نون • nuun

The letter *nuun* is pronounced like the *n* in the English word *nice*. It's a two-directional connector, so it connects on its right and left sides, and therefore it has all four potential forms. The initial and medial forms use the same shape as the *baa', taa', thaa',* and *yaa',* but the independent and final forms of the *nuun* are formed with a cuplike shape dipping beneath the line of writing. After writing the shape of the letter, you add a single dot above the character. Try them:

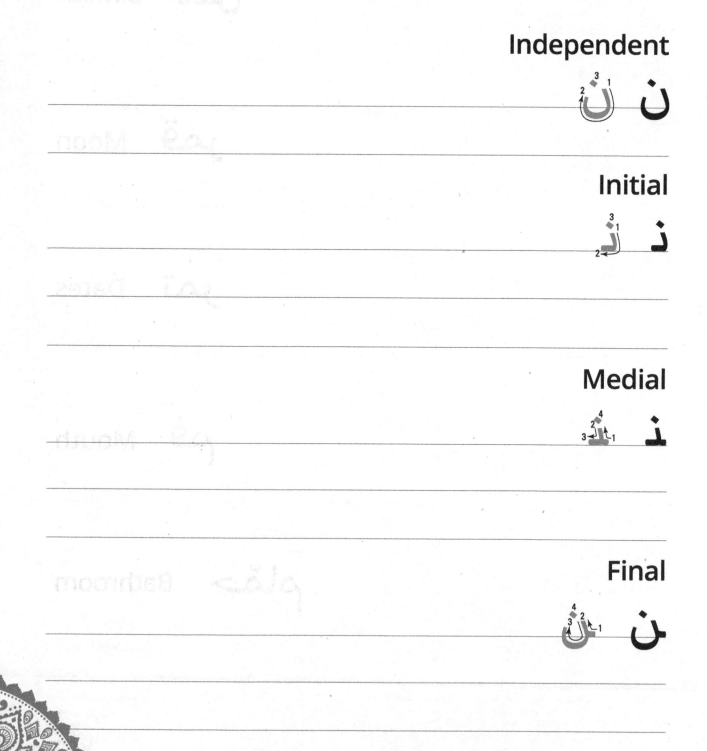

Independent

Initial

Medial

Final

Eagle نسر

نسر

At عند

عند

Daughter بنت

بنت

Belly بطن

بطن

Teeth أسنان

أسنان

haa' . هاء

The letter *haa'* is pronounced like the *h* in the English word *he*. It's a two-directional connector, so it connects on its right and left sides, and therefore it has all four potential forms. You will see below that the forms of the *haa'* can be quite different from one another depending on their position in the word; for instance, the independent form is like a zero, while the medial form is like a figure eight. Try them:

Independent

Initial

Medial

Final

Telephone هاتف

هاتف

ظهر Noon

ظهر

شهر Month

شهر

شبه Resemblance

شبه

شاه Shah/king (in chess)

شاه

taa' marbuuta · تاء مربوطة

The letter *taa' marbuuta* is a form that occurs only as the last letter of words, which are almost always feminine. You pronounce it as a final *a*. It is formed just like the *haa'*, but with two dots above it (just like a *taa'* would have). Try them:

Independent

ة

Final

ة

واو · # waaw

The letter *waaw* is pronounced like the *w* in the English word *we* or *u/oo* like the words *Zulu* or *balloon*. It's a one-directional connector, so it connects to a two-directional connector only on its own right side. It is formed like a large comma shape, with the bottom of the shape dipping below the line of writing. Try them:

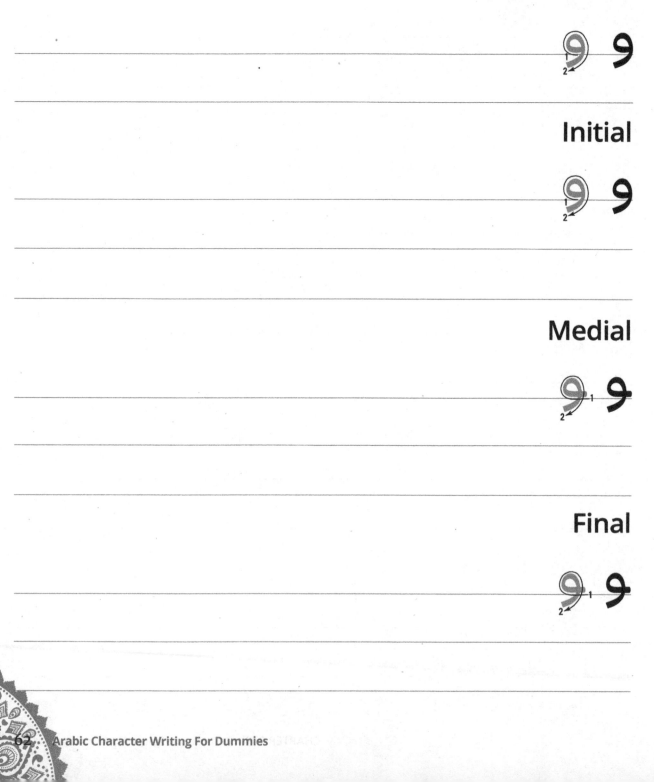

Independent

Initial

Medial

Final

مفردات

Practice

Homeland وطن

وطن

Voice صوت

صوت

Pardon عفو

عفو

Beans فول

فول

Enemy عدو

عدو

yaa' · ياء

The letter *yaa'* is pronounced like the *y* in the English word *yes* or a long *i* vowel, like the *ee* in the English word *seen*. It's a two-directional connector, so it connects on its right and left sides, and therefore it has all four potential forms. The initial and medial forms use the same shape as the *baa'*, *taa'*, *thaa'*, and *nuun*, but the independent and final forms of the *yaa'* are formed with an *s*-like shape dipping beneath the line of writing. After writing the shape of the letter, you add two dots below the character. Try them:

Independent

Initial

Medial

Final

مهارسة   Practice

Jasmine   ياسمين

ياسمين

Sheikh   شيخ

شيخ

Right   يمين

يمين

My pen   قلمي

قلمي

Tea   شاي

شاي

'alif maksuura · ألف مكسورة

The letter *'alif maksuura* is a form that occurs only as the last letter of words. You pronounce it as a final *a*. It is formed just like the *yaa'*, but without any dots. Practice the *'alif maksuura*.

Independent

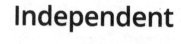

Final

Word	كلمة

كلمة

_____

Ball	كرة

كرة

_____

At	لدى

لدى

_____

Meaning	معنى

معنى

_____

_____

hamza · همزة

The *hamza* represents the sound linguists call the glottal stop. It is the sound sometimes occurring in American English with a *t* between two vowels, such as *Latin* (Laa'in) or *Batman* (Ba'man). In Arabic the *hamza* is written independently and also above or below the *'alif*, *waaw*, or *yaa'*. When appearing with the *hamza*, these letters are called *seats* of the hamza. Try them:

Independent

ع

'alif seat above

أ

'alif seat below

إ

waaw seat

ؤ

yaa' seat

ئ

Water ماء

ماء

To ask سأل

سأل

Islam إسلام

إسلام

Question سؤال

سؤال

Reader قارئ

قارئ

The Short Vowels الحركات

The *fatha* is a short line placed above a letter and is pronounced like the *a* in the word *ago*. Practice it with the letter *daal*, to produce the sound *da*.

دَ

_____

The *kasra* is a short line placed below a letter and is pronounced like the *i* in the word *bit*. Practice it with the letter *daal*, to produce the sound *di*.

دِ

_____

The *damma* is a small *waaw* placed above a letter and is pronounced like the *ou* in the word *soup*. Practice it with the letter *daal*, to produce the sound *du*.

دُ

_____

The *sukuun* is a small circle written above the letter to indicate that the letter has no vowel at all. Practice it with the letter *daal*.

دْ

_____

Additional Symbols

The *shadda* is like a small *W* shape written above a letter to indicate that the letter is doubled. Practice it with the letter *daal*.

دّ

Arabic writing does not permit two *'alifs* next to each other. So when you need to write two together, you instead write an *'alif* with a wavy line above it, known as a *madda*, as you can see below. Practice writing this.

آ

The Long Vowels حروف المدّ

The *'alif* is used to represent a long *a* vowel, similar to the *a* in the English word *cat*.
Practice it with the letter *daal*, to produce the sound *daa*.

دا دا

The *waaw* is used to represent a long *u* vowel, like the *oo* in the English word *boot*.
Practice it with the letter *daal*, to produce the sound *doo*.

دو دو

The *yaa'* is used to represent a long *i* vowel, like the *ee* in the English word *seen*.
Practice it with the letter *daal*, to produce the sound *dee*.

دي دي

Phrases in Arabic

What is your name and where do you live?

ما اِسْمُكَ وَأَيْنَ تَسْكُنُ؟

ما اِسْمُكَ وَأَيْنَ تَسْكُنُ؟

My name is...

اِسْمي...

اِسْمي...

How are you, Muhammad?

كَيْفَ حالُكَ يا مُحَمَّد ؟

كَيْفَ حالُكَ يا مُحَمَّد ؟

I write in Arabic.

أَكْتُب بِاللُّغَة اَلْعَرَبِيَّة.

أَكْتُب بِاللُّغَة اَلْعَرَبِيَّة.

Good morning

صَباح اَلْخَيْر

صَباح اَلْخَيْر

Good bye

مَعَ اَلسَّلامَة

مَعَ اَلسَّلامَة

I want to study Arabic.

أُريد أَن أَدْرُس اَللُّغَة اَلْعَرَبِيَّة.

أُريد أَن أَدْرُس اَللُّغَة اَلْعَرَبِيَّة.

Are you happy?

هَل أَنْتَ مَسْرور؟

هَل أَنْتَ مَسْرور؟

The Numbers الأَعْداد

١.	وَاحِدٌ	وَاحِدٌ
٢.	إِثْنَانِ	إِثْنَانِ
٣.	ثَلاَثَةٌ	ثَلاَثَةٌ
٤.	أَرْبَعَةٌ	أَرْبَعَةٌ
٥.	خَمْسَةٌ	خَمْسَةٌ
٦.	سِتَّةٌ	سِتَّةٌ
٧.	سَبْعَةٌ	سَبْعَةٌ
٨.	ثَمَانِيَةٌ	ثَمَانِيَةٌ
٩.	تِسْعَةٌ	تِسْعَةٌ
١٠.	عَشَرَةٌ	عَشَرَةٌ

The Numbers   الأعداد

Appendix

Extra Practice Pages

Arabic Character Writing For Dummies

Arabic Character Writing For Dummies

Arabic Character Writing For Dummies

Arabic Character Writing For Dummies